# DUNES REVIEW

Cover art, "Heaped," by Skye Livingston.

DUNES REVIEW (ISSN: 1545-3111) is published biannually by
Michigan Writers, Inc., and with the generous contributions of our Patrons.

# EDITORIAL BOARD

| | |
|---|---|
| SENIOR EDITOR | Jennifer Yeatts |
| MANAGING EDITOR | Tanya Muzumdar |
| READERS | Kevin Avery |
| | Jim Crockett |
| | Melissa Fournier |
| | Tanya Muzumdar |
| | Emma Smith |
| | Sarah Wangler |
| FOUNDING EDITOR | Anne-Marie Oomen |
| ADVISORY SUPPORT | Anne-Marie Oomen |
| PRODUCTION ASSISTANCE | Barbara Hodge |

# GRATITUDE TO OUR GENEROUS PATRONS:

*Sharon Angel*

*Chuck Corson, BLK MRKT Coffee*

*Mandy Gibson, Certified Quickbooks Advisor, "Helping edit the other kind of books"*

*Jennifer Kirkpatrick Johnson*

*Susan Odgers and the free, weekly NMC Writing Workshop for Writers Experienced With Homelessness*

*Daniel W. Stewart*

*Joe and Lana Volpe*

# DUNES REVIEW

VOLUME 19, ISSUE I

## CONTENTS

| | | |
|---|---|---|
| 1 | Jennifer Yeatts | *Editor's Note* |

**William J. Shaw Memorial Prize for Poetry**

| | | |
|---|---|---|
| 2 | Constance Reinhard | **First Place**, *Malum et Bonum* |
| 3 | Brendan Straubel | **Second Place**, *Waxwing* |
| 5 | Robb Astor | **Third Place**, *Dear* |

| | | |
|---|---|---|
| 6 | Greg Jensen | *Here are the People* |
| 7 | Andrew Collard | *Dressing up for Church* |
| 9 | Zilka Joseph | *Fire: For Beginners* |
| 11 | Greg Jensen | *I Used to See Cowboys* |
| 12 | Nicco Pandolfi | *A Eulogy for Socrates* |
| 13 | Janice Zerfas | *The Dead Woman Looked Above Her* |
| 15 | Lillo Way | *Great Blue* |
| 16 | Todd Mercer | *Midway Airport Plot Point* |
| 17 | Andrew Collard | *Newly Hollowed* |
| 18 | Zilka Joseph | *Bees, Sunday Brunch* |
| 20 | Julie Stotz-Ghosh | *Owl in Night* |
| 21 | Zilka Joseph | *The Blessed* |
| 23 | Elaine McIntosh | *We Hid* |
| 24 | Suzanne Shumway | *The Light the Whisky Brings* |
| 27 | Kathleen Diane Nolan | *Crash* |
| 28 | Greg Jensen | *Peninsulas* |
| 30 | Janice Zerfas | *The Dead Woman Knew How to Float* |
| 32 | Jeffrey Alfier | *Two at Gunnison Beach* |
| 33 | Kirk Westphal | *Eden* |
| 34 | Greg Jensen | *Quicksilver* |

| | | |
|---|---|---|
| 35 | Kathleen Diane Nolan | *Outside, the Country* |
| 36 | Dave Hardin | *Bullets Pass Through* |
| 41 | Lillo Way | *April First* |
| 42 | Todd Mercer | *Rust Belt Anniversary* |
| 43 | Karen Anderson | *Blessings* |
| 44 | Diane Henningfeld | *Wisconsin Triolet: My Future Mother-in-law Teaches Me to Play Sheepshead* |
| 45 | Greg Jensen | *Skin* |
| 46 | Kelley Jean White | *Sick Little Peach Girl* |
| 47 | Ed Coletti | *Marionette* |
| 48 | Ed Coletti | *Hypatia of Alexandria* |
| 49 | Elaine McIntosh | *The Green Dress* |
| 50 | Ellen Stone | *Milk Pitcher* |
| 51 | Stefen Holtrey | *To John Keats* |
| 52 | Ellen Stone | *Driving to Galesburg* |
| 53 | Diane Henningfeld | *Turning* |
| 54 | Kathleen Diane Nolan | *Brass* |
| 55 | Robert Earle | *No Regrets?* |
| 62 | *Acknowledgements, Contributor Notes* | |
| 66 | *Call for Patrons* | |
| 67 | *Submissions, subscriptions and Michigan Writers membership information* | |

# Editor's Note

*Our nature compels us to hold tightly to the things that bring us joy. People, places, simple objects that act as metaphor for some weighty experience we've had—we covet them. Even when they begin to slip away from us, we try our best to hang on.*

*But of course the slipping away is certain. Sooner or later, not that you need a poet to tell you: things end. Experiences come to a close, people move on, whether elsewhere in this world or into another. We often regret these endings, wishing we could remain in the places we love with the people who have shaped us into ourselves. We are told not to linger in the past, to move on, to live in the present. Humbug, I say. Our pasts are rich with the pains and delights that have made us who we are. To honor and cherish the symbols of our past lives is not to discount the beauty of the present. Ellen Stone's "Milk Pitcher" and Elaine McIntosh's "Green Dress" remind us that some remnants of our histories are worthy of preservation.*

*As usual, the opposite is also true. Letting go is cathartic, liberating, healing. In Andrew Collard's "Newly Hollowed" (one of the best break-up poems I've ever read), tulips bloom with nobody watching, a symbol of new life beyond a ruined relationship. Janice Zerfas' dead woman poems—meditations, really—give us a character who learns, at the end of the end, to* let regret go.

*Bodies of water float their way through this issue, washing away debris, carrying loved ones away, carrying us away and mirroring our pensive faces. A permanent impermanence, waves pulse and change constantly within a fixed periphery. As you make your way through these pages, I hope you'll dive beneath the surface. Look down deep to shadowy mysteries below, then up to a sky that waits to reclaim your breath. Feel the current shift back and forth and back again.*

—Jennifer Yeatts

WILLIAM J. SHAW MEMORIAL PRIZE FOR POETRY:
FIRST PLACE

## Constance Reinhard
## *MALUM ET BONUM*

Soon after the mal-
ady was confirmed
some pols saw it as a bon-
anza for their side and
started to mal-
ign the President, who
sent soldiers on a bon
voyage to help contain the virus,
but the media knows that mal-
content sells newspapers
so they downplayed the bon
mots about difficult transmission
and emphasized instead mal-
feasance by patient and hospital.
Meanwhile even the bona
fide liberals like us cancelled our trips
and did not counter the mal-
edictions against the nurse
who traveled sick or le bon
médecin from Doctors without Borders
who returned home with the mal-
evolent virus inside.  Meanwhile,
in Africa, the bon-
ny patients aid each other, and those
Americans who help despite mal-
ice from their fellow citizens
increase the world's store of bon-
homie and remind the rest of us
that loving kindness is primal.

WILLIAM J. SHAW MEMORIAL PRIZE FOR POETRY:
SECOND PLACE

## Brendan Straubel
*WAXWING*

By twilight the day of the funeral
only my two uncles are left.
We sit on the bank above the river,
taking rare pulls from our warm beers.
Saying nothing. Watching
the turkeys rise up to roost, one by one.
Each clumsy in its flight
but ordered, rhythmic, nonetheless,
one by one, into the high branches of the hardwoods.

Finally, I pick up the over-sized Mason jar,
run my finger up its side. Plain.
Heavy glass. Thick rubber gasket.
Metal Latch.
He kept his sugar here.
For coffee and tea.
I press it against my hip and navigate the drop to the river.
Above me the turkeys rile.
Beat their wings, pace their perches.

I wade the willow-strained eddy.
Chat and sand bounce across my dress shoes.
A dark salmon, glass-eyed and trailed by gray
flags of flesh, rolls above a gravel bar nearby.
I say a few words. Of family and fate.
And this river's constant push toward open water.

At the base of the eddy, I open the make-shift urn,
tip it toward the water
and now

the ashes of my father

flow with the Betsie,

glowing impossibly gold in some sliver of light.
They divide and reform, spin and swirl, expand and contract,
pulsing in the same powerful ropes and rolling braids
as a band of Cedar

Waxwing

Thrown as one into flight,
startled by the unseen.

WILLIAM J. SHAW MEMORIAL PRIZE FOR POETRY:
THIRD PLACE

## Robb Astor
*DEAR*

But you already *have* changed the world
don't you see?
The young Japanese mother
struggling with her stroller,
so many thoughtless people,
I stopped to let her pass
and, for some reason, bowed.
When she bowed back
everything fell apart.
I found myself wandering among the crowd
falling in love with someone I didn't know.
It wasn't her.
I'm in love with everyone now.

## Greg Jensen
### *HERE ARE THE PEOPLE*

When you steeple your fingers
in front of your face
nobody who walks by

asks if the sermon
today is different.
They can't hear your bare

knuckles cracking
on the crowded street
or who is speaking

in tongues.
Someone inside
lights a candle

then hums a hymn.
Your bus fare
is a fire burning

out of control.
You think it is all gone,
then the flames start over.

## Andrew Collard
*DRESSING UP FOR CHURCH*

The steeple only reaches
      so high: a boy can
almost believe
      the clouds have met it
halfway, as he runs
      through decisive rain

to where the deacons
      hold open ancient
doors. A bit of charcoal,
      smeared on by his mother,
washes from cheek to
      ratty t-shirt, the Cheetos

soggy in his makeshift
      bindle. A sign reads
Hobo Night above the fellowship
      hall's threshold, the Wednesday
night children's program
      already commenced.

The kids pose for pictures
      by the door to the empty
food bank, and race between
      corners at an elder's
whistle. The same sound
      gathers them to hear

the message: first that none
      are righteous, no not
one; and then, the words
      of comfort, God works
for the good of those
      who love him, good news

to the poor. An hour unreels, and
      walking out, the boy
almost emerges, his shirt

        catching on an exposed nail.
He looks to the parking
        lot across the street:

the department store's
        shopping carts corralled
and orderly, fixed into place
        like a mask
as the clouds, silent,
        disperse without a will.

## Zilka Joseph
*FIRE: FOR BEGINNERS*

                Breathe in deep and blow
softly as if drying wet clay,
and spell it out,

say *faaah* —like a

long cry of pain;

            then say i
(pronounced eye),
pushed with force —

like Adam and Eve
by a blood-red sirocco,

expelled
by the seraph
hot with holy rage;

            next say *ire*,

let your tongue lash
the virgin
syllable of

anger —
           orphan of fear
and heart-break searching for
a name. What lesson

this? Divine

disillusion? Light gone
wrong? What being
could not contain

the raging
           conflagration? In wrath,

desire, dreams and ash live
the alpha and omega

of flame. Burnt child, see these scars!
We are all branded young.

## Greg Jensen
### *I USED TO SEE COWBOYS*

I used to see cowboys
when I squinted
at the ceiling
throwing curlicues of ropes
through the clouds.

When their lassos fell,
I pulled up close
to the head of a pony,
his shoulders twitching
and growing tame

beneath me.
I put a bit in his mouth,
nails in his hooves,
and cinched a saddle
around his swollen belly.

These days I see a rope
and feel my burdens
getting loose.
I can't catch them anymore
around the neck.

## Nicco Pandolfi
### *A EULOGY FOR SOCRATES*

We must learn to sleep with the knowledge
That we may never know the songs of bygone birds,
Or divine the midnight fears of bears.
We are left to seesaw through a spinning world,
Pursuing truth like some common ancestor long extinct,
Forever rearranging its fossilized bones
In a dusty museum back room.
Certainty is a comfort enjoyed exclusively by
Yesterday's disciples, stoically composing their brows
Just so, anticipating every portrait.
The rest of us live in a world not of answers,
But of questions begetting more questions
With the alarming fecundity of Catholics.
Socrates knew answers ring false as broken bells
And preferred to converse in ever-rising inflection,
His voice circling high as a falcon
Seeking wispy purchase in the clouds.
But he drank hemlock for his curiosity,
Which hardly recommends it to those of us
Looking forward to the blamelessness of age,
With its wheezy parade of rocking chair fibs.

Janice Zerfas
## THE DEAD WOMAN LOOKED ABOVE HER

1.

When the dead woman looked above her, she saw Canadian goose decoys with wings wide as awnings.

At first the dead woman thought she was under an awning, but shadows glided along.

She could hear the thrumming of their heartbeats, the watery rays she was settling under.

They made more darkness, a crevasse in the sky, a pointed emblem, a sign pointing to absence, then absconding.

The dead woman liked most was the ripple of the cachet of wings above her.

Such a silly goose, the dead woman thought of herself, just sitting there feeling the swell of the geese above her as though raking black dirt.

There must be a better way of looking at the world above her: she could look up at a graying tree stand, wintry packing crates, choke cherry parabolas, flagrant sumac, the burl of a tree for a gun stock.

What about the decoy poised above the shed, as if it could lift the wooden structure with a quick uplift and little friction?

No matter what happened, they were a delightful social gathering, especially the selvage of their wings, the cut of the wing as if from a zoot soot.

They were also unexpected, and surely didn't see the dead woman sitting at the picnic table is if her pose made a signature.

To the dead woman, all the rippling geese crossing over were a sign: branches had lignified, corn thickened into saddlebags, apples accreted into jade or ruby or garnets.

To the dead woman, the geese modeled a living flight, greyer than towing chains.

2.
The dead woman believed that their wings rushed by like small talk.
If she could stand on the picnic table, she would be able to touch them as easily as the rungs of a curved apple ladder.
If she could have seen them earlier, she would have got into position.
Who was she to know it would happen so quickly, and disappear like fingerprints?
There was nothing to do but wait, hope the geese dark as fuel oil will sound again.
There was really nothing to do, but wonder at the way they reordered the sky.
Silly goose, the dead woman knocked herself, it's the heron that's the calming bird, not the flock of geese, lightly burned paper, above her.

## Lillo Way
*GREAT BLUE*

Heron, why have you, crotchety old man,
        stalked me, lithe young woman,
stretched your neck over me
        and watched – unmoving
unmoved in your absolute possession?

You, still as a woodcut until
        your shaggy-sparse overcomb
fluffs loose in the swampwind.
        You'll wait forever
if it takes forever.

You, for whom flying is to unfold painstakingly
        ancient wings hardly yours –
your ancestors' wings torn, worn
        rags of gray and dirty blue, uncranked –
my breath comes short as I glimpse you drop them
        impossibly heavy then barely
haul them up again.

You, who exaggerate those skinny legs
        to walk the shore as twigs
would walk were they able
        until underbelly deep, you meditate
before your lightning strike.

Why have you staked your weirdness
        into my neck knees heart, my hollow bones,
my salt grass hair?

## Todd Mercer
### *MIDWAY AIRPORT PLOT POINT*

He could only go as far as Midway. There the doors to everywhere else opened and the thousands swallowed her up. Midway implying pivot, balance between terminal points. Where were the architects referencing? Halfway from The Loop to Joliet? Cali to New York?

Gone away versus being here now. After Midway she and he became mutual abstractions, icons, voicemail phantoms, static as photographs for the separation's run.

Before it she'd ask, "Are we almost there?" an echo of the question for her father in childhood. "These are the Early Days," the father would say. No, the husband. One, both. She's forever merging memories.

In (or possibly before) the Early Days, her father was a beautiful man, a deeply flawed man. She knows each person can be. Isn't and is.

The husband aimed all the way back, banking on the gasoline to stretch. Tri-State to the Frank Borman. Indiana Tollway to an overloaded highway, to a doze-y one, to the Gerald Ford. To the driveway, hopefully. Odometer math is weak compared to the magic that will make her reappear at the Curbside Pickup.

Today he's a voicemail phantom, a haunt, largely theoretical amidst road-hum. Quiet car to a silent house in semi-suspension.

She's an hour into the abstraction phase. Five hundred knots with a continuous vapor trail, fanning into cirrus clouds, wispy.

## Andrew Collard
### *NEWLY HOLLOWED*

The nest is lint-tufts and fragments of a Kit Kat wrapper, stuffed into a
rotting corner of the porch's ceiling. Wind repels the approaching finch,
plastic bag inflated from her beak like a parachute. I like to think the
garbage pile amassing on the floorboards lives in service to her, a little
less scavenging in the wetness of an opening world. Someone used
to live here

>before the house fell into heaving silence: conversations
turned serious, the birds flew startled from their coves

heading south. I'd forgotten what it was to sleep alone, unfolding into
spaces newly hollowed. First, books piled on the couch, the shelves
slowly emptying; then flies infested the cat-box, occasionally winding
towards unwashed dishes in the kitchen sink.

>I like to think the nest is incomplete, as I read wrapped in
blankets big enough to share. But socks left on the carpet speak
like tea leaves:

>>a mess of comfort built
on remnants of another's
home,

>>and nothing's missing

>>as outside, tulips open
unobserved.

## Zilka Joseph
### *BEES, SUNDAY BRUNCH*

How easily you boasted (you who
rarely brag) as you poured the amarone,
about your victory,

the beehive

that grew into a city inside the lip
of the fancy brick façade
beneath your window;

your kind face suddenly split into smiles,
into many planes (like a Picasso
painting), and pointing you explained

how the cancerous hive had grown—
and how impossible, at first,
it had been to get to its humming

heart; so sweet the moment was, you said,

when the vacuum cleaner
sucked out the hidden cells,
the golden lives, the royal jelly,

the sudden burst of energy that filled you,

when your finger pressed the power button
(like God's finger touching Adam's
in the blue of the Sistine sky). It was good

you said, to watch the broken beads
in the stream of honey and crushed
wax pulsing through the translucent pipe.

And then when it was done, the twisted rope
of furry shapes you flung like a dead
serpent into the thicket beyond your tidy lawn—
the strange chain of lifeless bodies

and debris of vanquished city
breaking in air as it fell, —

was it heavier than you thought?

## Julie Stotz-Ghosh
*OWL IN NIGHT*

I wake to almost silence, a hollow
call in the darkness. I wake
and find my voice has gone.

It is not sickness, though, that
draws me to the window, to open
locks and let in icy air,

sky obscured by grayness.
The sound is real, a great-horned
owl, or two, and me. My breath.

The window pane is cool and
soothes my head as I rest my arms
and chin and listen.

I listen so hard I hear my blood
move between what is now patterned
repetition of call and silence and call.

I think I might see this owl on
darkened branches of bare trees
as what little light that lives opens

more windows for me. I think I might
see all the way across the field, see mice
and wild turkey asleep beneath brown

corn stalks, if that is what they do.
I think I hear footsteps on frosted
grass, shush shush, and I

imagine deer, and myself, on the icy
path toward something in that darkness.

## Zilka Joseph
### *THE BLESSED*

wings still glossy, she's slouched

in the shade of the marauding fig
wild roots swallowing
cracked bricks

at the lip of our kitchen window
she waits, lopsided

tail ragged
as if rat-bitten

gaze deeper than hunger

my hands scrape down my plate
some meat I leave on the bones
extra grains of rice

she hops near
balancing this edge

who will care for us, little sister
we who are broken but not by our own hands

tap-tapping her beak
she picks cleanly

it's for bullies I keep watch
my eyes scour the sun-white rectangle of sky

small cousin of the rook
and of the hard-beaked raven
how cruel are our kind

do we not bleed do we not die
we are not ravaged by fury but fear

so eat at my house, my one-eyed beauty
rest here then O bent-bodied bird

my wild, starved, one-legged one

# Elaine McIntosh
## *WE HID*

alone
in our rooms
hid my mother's bruises
from neighbor questions
hid liquor and money
hid the rage, gone
from home too young
hid yearnings from our lovers
hid sadness in our bodies-
each heart-life masked,
squinting for the light.

## Suzanne Rosenthal Shumway
### *THE LIGHT THE WHISKY BRINGS*

With names like Hop, Bully, and T.J., my uncles were bound to be characters. As a small child, I loved having relatives with such distinctive names; I felt proud of them, as if I belonged to a special family that had somehow earned the right to bestow such outlandish monikers on its members. My own nicknames were fairly predictable for a red-haired tomboy: "Red" or "Firewagon." But it was my Uncle Travis who gave me the name that stuck. To Uncle Travis, I was always "Tiger," and as Tiger, I followed him everywhere: to the hardware store, to the feed store, and to the gas station he owned with his brother, my Uncle Bob, where I pumped gas for grizzled men in dented Chevy pick-ups, men who chewed tobacco, drank Pearl beer, and smiled at the spectacle of a seven-year-old girl managing a gas pump.

I always knew that Uncle Travis was a drinker, and I knew just as surely that he didn't handle his liquor well. My mother's siblings were divided into two sorts: those who handled their liquor poorly, and those who never touched a drop. Uncle Travis was the poster child of the drinking siblings: a sloppy and emotional drunk who might just as easily break out into tears as into fisticuffs. He was a real cowboy, Texan through and through, but he loved me and let me follow him around on those summer days when we were visiting.

Uncle Travis had a friend named Shot Smith. I never asked why he was called "Shot"; perhaps having a slew of uncles with odd names had predisposed me to refrain from asking too many questions about names. I did, however, ask about Shot's left ear, which was only half there. It didn't show that much when he wore his cowboy hat, but indoors, when he took it off (because no Texan ever wears his hat inside), it was clear that the top part of his ear had gone missing, leaving his head looking lopsided, as if he'd gotten a haircut from a barber suffering from a bad case of vertigo. Shot, whose leathery face was lined even in those days, grinned when he told me that a cow had bitten it off. I never thought to doubt that answer until I mentioned it, many years later, to my mother, who laughed outright. "He was in a car accident," she said. "He'd been drinking." Certainly that made more sense than the idea of a cow biting off his ear, I realized, and then wondered why I had never questioned Shot's story. Why would a cow bite off a man's ear, anyway?

What would one have to do to a cow to make it angry enough to bite an ear? And, as long as he was making up stories, why pick on a hapless cow to appoint the culprit? Why not at least choose a fierce, snorting bull? But in those days I was satisfied with simple answers.

On one particular summer afternoon, Uncle Travis and Shot invited me to go on a drive with them, so I hopped into Uncle Travis's truck, crawled between them on the bench seat, and we took off, driving on dusty county roads, past stands of scrubby mesquite trees and ragged herds of cattle, until we had left Dallas far behind us. It was one of those broiling summer days so common in Texas, when the heat rises up from the road in front of you in waves, making it look like a worn and tired ribbon shimmering in a non-existent breeze. We turned on to smaller and smaller roads, until at last we pulled onto a gravel lane, then up to a tiny ramshackle house that might have been white many years before.

I'm not sure why we stopped at that abandoned farmhouse. Perhaps Shot and Uncle Travis were picking up something for a friend; maybe they were just checking on someone's hunting lease as a favor. I do know that we went straight into the kitchen like we owned the place and sat down at a Formica kitchen table left over from the 1950s, with green edging and seat cushions to match. Then Uncle Travis stood up and began to rummage around in the cupboards until he found a bottle that was two-thirds empty. He unscrewed the lid and poured the liquor into two milk glasses, leaving the bottle on the counter. He sat down, handed one of the glasses to Shot, and they each took a swig.

"Is there anything I can drink?" The dust and heat had made me thirsty, and I was hoping for a Dr. Pepper. Shot and Uncle Travis exchanged a glance, and then Shot walked over to the cupboard, opened it, and pulled out a tiny glass jigger. Uncle Travis scooted one of the chairs over to the sink and motioned me over with a sideways movement of his head. "Come on, Tiger," he said, and that was enough. I trotted over and clambered up on the chair. I couldn't have been more than seven or eight years old.

I watched as Shot poured the golden liquid into tiny glass, tipping the neck of the bottle with such care that the jigger filled up imperceptibly, as if by magic. In that moment, as the whisky oozed its way into the shot glass, the sunlight flowed through the smeared window above the kitchen sink, a bright and insistent summer light, yet gentle as the dust motes that danced all around me. Standing on the chair, I held my hand out for the glass, but Uncle Travis stopped me.

"Let's set you up here," he said, knowing how I would react to my first taste of whisky. He lifted me up onto the counter, and I sat there, my feet inside the stainless steel sink, my dusty sneakers tapping against its bottom, sounding a tattoo of exotic expectation. At last Shot held the jigger out to me, and my small fingers closed around the glass.

"It's redeye, isn't it, Uncle Travis?" I asked, using the term he had taught me, one that real cowpokes used. I looked up over my shoulder at him. He smiled, but I knew he was looking more at Shot than at me. I raised the glass to my lips and tipped it back, drinking it in one gulp, as all the cowboys did in the old westerns I had seen.

I tried to swallow, but my throat exploded in flames, and I wheezed for breath. At the same time, whisky sprayed from my mouth and nose, and I realized then why I was sitting on the sink: droplets of whisky went everywhere. Somewhere beyond the pain, I could hear Shot's low growl of laughter, and I felt Uncle Travis's left hand tighten on my shoulder as his right hand patted me on the back. It took me a few minutes to catch my breath, and when I did, I looked up at Uncle Travis through watering—but not tearful—eyes. He smiled, his own blue eyes shining, but I could tell he was proud of me for not crying, and in that moment, I forgave him for his part in the joke.

## Kathleen Diane Nolan
*CRASH*

Mosquitoes clotted on the screen.
Air thick like paste. My father, drunk,
yanking dresser drawers,
                              snapping gold hinges
on the suitcase.

Yelling at my mother as he left
*You could spoil a high mass.*

Chasing his Plymouth down the road with my sisters,
                              stones caught in our sandals.

*Daddy, Daddy,*
until the car was out of sight.

The next morning. Coffee, orange juice, a chance of showers.
Paper sack lunches, coins for milk in balled-up

napkins. My father at the kitchen table reading the *Daily News*.

The deaf girl from next door, knocking, leading
me outside by the hand,
from the broken shingles
to the dented car and back, pointing,

pointing. *Your father*, she signed at me.
No, no, I said.
                              He didn't.
                              He did not.

And I stood there staring,
staring at the crack in the house,

staring until it disappeared.

## Greg Jensen
### *PENINSULAS*

I am floating
in the Sound,

chills pulsing through me
surrounded by dead

fish eyes looking up
caught in a gelid bloom,

like starlight
in a shot glass.

I feel myself drifting
between peninsulas

where the fog hangs
low in the trees.

The pupil fixes itself
when it stares too long

at the vexing world
crashing around it.

The more I know the more
constricted I become.

Bodhidharma sat and faced a wall
for nine consecutive years.

The wall eventually showed
hairline cracks.

I want to lie down again
and be held from below

like the monk who penetrated
his confusion without

a word coming
or going on the sea

where his whole mind rested.

Janice Zerfas
## THE DEAD WOMAN KNEW HOW TO FLOAT

1.

When the dead woman knew she could float like a black walnut, she felt excited.
Sensing the glance of a heron on the river bank, the dead woman was glad she was heavy as a salmon.
The dead woman bobbed in the water for hours, rippling around the cachet of lines.
Sometimes she saw waders hip boots, lines cast not netting the catalpa seed pods, mirrored reflections of bulbous faces from above peering down without seeing her.
She saw the man with a face wrinkled as a clump of shoe laces, hiding the undersize walleye and sucker in a trash bag.
Couldn't they stop throwing canned corn at her, thinking she was a trailing carp?
Once in a while, conversations floated by, making her laugh when she saw condoms filling with the current.
Once, she saw the leaves do a polka above her.
Sometimes she preferred hearing the geese thrush.
She doesn't need much now that she is like a black walnut, the shell flaking away like pie crust.
She liked listening to the sound of the rain hit the water, the scud of a raccoon's claws.
She bobs more easily now that the barometric pressure has changed, now that the weather is cooler, never liked the wind from the east.
Only a wind from the south meant that bait was headed for a mouth.

If she gave just a small filigree to someone finding her by chance, would someone know to paint an animal trap with the odor?
She liked resting and looking at the clouds doodling above, thin as baking soda.
Why hadn't she cascaded into a bay near the abandoned boat launch she slid along?
The dead woman doesn't choose sides between the sand bar and the rocks, the sand bar and the white poplar ghost tree with its skin sanded with stars rain sun moon.
Her nakedness no longer embarrassing, she turned her buttocks to ripple like double walnuts.
Turning herself on her side, she wondered why the skin under her flesh was crumbling into black tobacco skein. To the dead woman, the sound of the siren warning nearby waders the dam gates were opening was a sign of heaven.
The dead woman is the wide tail of the river.

2.

The dead woman knew if the current was more than 7 or 8 knots, then swim toward the bouys if she wanted to get to the island.
At regret's end, she was going to give up picking up all the trash floating by her: speckled fishing bait luminescent as nail polish, embalmed fast food boxes always yellow.
She liked especially fallen leaves already golden caught in the water, like a flitting sun or a forehead.
She could feel when the river turned over, ready to become colder.
She knew when it was time to let regret go.

## Jeffrey Alfier
### *TWO AT GUNNISON BEACH*

November, and the ocean under faultless skies
sends men hustling to reclaim their fishing
grounds like flame finding wood. Hooks baited

with sandworms and mossbunker,
their faith's in the breaking strength of nylon line
—scripted arcs that climb briefly the seamless

Atlantic air above False Hook Channel,
hope for a grand catch out of what nears
the shore from shipwrecks and deeper waters.

They stand amid the soft decay of the sea
—the horseshoe crabs and broken ark shells
washed underfoot in salt demise.

They hang for hours at the lip of the solid
world before the day relinquishes to dusk, lines
reeled-in, a dozen striper they'll soon divvy up

on the cooler's ice. Bourbon is uncorked.
Soft talk bleeds away with the last light.
Tired bodies lift from folding chairs

as they leave in their own cars, each one
asking himself what he could have said
to make the other stay a bit longer, facing the sea.

## Kirk Westphal
### *EDEN*

I know a Bridge between an Orchard and a Lake,
between the lifting down of apple weight
and resurrection of the limbs,
between the outstretched years of applewood
and driftwood, new each morning,
One cupped hand of earth
on either side.
I sleep within the Orchard
and you beside the Lake
but it is your flesh beneath the fruit skin,
my palm beneath the waves,
your leafy eyes upon me,
my touch emulsified.
If this was Holy Water,
If these were Trees of Life,
Hands, the Bridge.
Words, the River.

# Greg Jensen
## *QUICKSILVER*

The pond is a smooth surface
boiling with bugs
in the summer.

How many legs kick
the air getting hotter.
A swimmer dives

under the glass
feeling his way.
Held down by a mirror

gathering shadows
like quicksilver rolling
in a petri dish.

He pumps his legs
and looks up.
There is no other world

waiting to see
if he makes it back
from under this sky

whose shadows never leave
the rocks he'd thrown overhead
from a field

always buzzing
in his ears.

## Kathleen Diane Nolan
### *OUTSIDE, THE COUNTRY*

Like ghosts walking into
the old church's basement,
my father and his friends came
to tell their stories,
to pull shards of glass
from each other's feet, to pray.

Even the ones
who didn't believe
in God seemed to crave
some taste of mercy.
They counted days
and hours, passed

a basket from lap
to lap to pay for coffee
and cake for someone
sober a year, for someone
back from relapse.
Outside, the country

between the willing
and the unwilling spread,
vast and gray, littered with moss,
branches and bones.
Outside, the earthly self
and its tangled walk home.

In the end, a few of them wandered
off looking for a bar, a beer,
a shot of whisky. Others stayed
and swept the floor, emptied
the trash. Some lingered, stacking
and restacking the chairs in a corner.

## Dave Hardin
### *BULLETS PASS THROUGH*

> *And you shall know them by their cloaks of cobalt flame stitched with rivers of gold, and bullets shall pass through them as ghosts through all our remaining days.*

It's the coat I remember. The flapping tails proclaimed him, splayed hood the filthy halo of a holy fool. Zipper-shot, the color of tinned meat, his name written in the collar in Sharpie: Collis Flowers. My hand closed over the crude block lettering a split second before I pulled him out of traffic on Eureka Avenue.

The coat was easy to spot in the backlit elbows at the ends of the long hallways of the Haphouse Skills Center where Collis attended school. It was shapeless in the way an untethered tarpaulin on a windy job site floats out of your field of vision. In another life the coat might have harbored a dog-eared passport or a nickel-plated revolver or a diamond ring in a hinged velvet box. Instead, the torn pockets concealed twists of paper, unremarkable stones, packets of Heinz catsup, and shit fashioned into fussy little beads. These curated treasures were known only to me and a few other teachers.

There wasn't a classroom that could hold him, armored in that coat. He spent crowded days sparring with the voices in his head. A grandee greeting people up and down the hall, he was a familiar fixture, cadging coffee in a tired Styrofoam cup, slouching in doorways, haunting the main entrance.

Collis lived at the nearby state-run Ragland Regional Center. It was a train-table layout of identical brick cottages scattered over weedy tundra speared by a few anemic trees. The whole package was tied loosely by a meandering ring road. Every so often a beefy security guard in a compact sedan, torso crisscrossed with belts and lanyards, made a lazy circumnavigation. The steel doors to the cottage Collis called home had thick glass windows reinforced with metal mesh and locked from both sides. The few times I'd been inside had been enough. I had no desire to return.

The Friday morning of the Eureka Road incident, Collis was on his way to celebrating a quiet week in relative compliance with his behavior plan, a non-binding contract he couldn't read and hadn't been asked to sign. I decided to reward him by arranging breakfast off campus at his favorite restaurant, Six Stars; American owned, ask about our daily specials! It was a mild late winter day, a good excuse to get out of the building for a couple of hours. For company I invited a colleague, Mike Bauer and another student, Jimmy Dubois. We should have known better.

On the best of days Jimmy was unpredictable, a bottle of nitroglycerin on a corduroy road. Collis was no less explosive, but a close observer would sense a slight barometric spike signaling bad weather ahead. Collis had goodwill to spare but not enough to overcome roiling mental illness, an orca of utter fear that could swallow him whole without provocation. Midway through pancakes swimming in canned strawberries and whipped cream, bruised clouds began massing over his brow. I watched the storm approaching fast in the tiny screens of his eyes.

There hadn't been time to call for the check or take one last sip of coffee or activate a back-up plan, had we been smart enough to make one. Collis exploded like a champagne cork. He had me by two good strides, twenty years my junior and surprisingly fit for a damaged human being reared in institutions. He hit the door, only sidewalk and a ribbon of blasted grass between him and the busy thoroughfare.

It's the coat I remember. I threw out a hand, aiming for the hood, cowl of a mad monk. It occurred to me that this was what they meant, movie cops bragging about making a collar. Cars blew by on Eureka Avenue, inches away from where we lay entwined, safe on the narrow verge.

Bauer and Jimmy followed us outside. Bauer helped me drag Collis out of harm's way. I sandwiched him facing the wall of the diner, binding his arms to his sides. Collis, momentarily stunned by my clumsy tackle, revived spectacularly bellowing like a Cossack, trying his best to break my hold, make a run for daylight. By now cars were slowing for a look-see and I noticed the surprised faces of former fellow diners through the big plate glass window. Maybe it was the spectacle of a middle-aged white man restraining a young, enraged black man, or Jimmy hot footing it on the sidewalk enraptured by the gathering jazz. We had captured everyone's attention.

The waitress appeared. I was moved by her willingness to be of use, but only momentarily. She handed the check to Bauer and glared at Collis and me, pressed up against the warming brick.

Jimmy, leaping about like a magpie, crowed over and over again, "hey baby, hey baby, hey baby!"

An elderly man approached from the parking lot, fists clenched. Everyone stopped for a moment, baffled by the unscripted introduction of a new character in our morning farce. Jimmy, inspired perhaps by new narrative possibilities, unleashed a corrosive stream of profanity strong enough to pit pig iron.

The man took a step closer and said, "Looks like you fellas beatin' on a black guy."

The ambiguity of the man's statement confused me. Good Samaritan or geriatric vigilante, offering to lend a hand in commission of a heinous crime? Eventually he seemed to lose all resolve to give in to the urgings of his better or lesser angels and stalked into the restaurant. By then a small crowd had gathered. Bauer held up his wrist and pointed at his watch. He opened and closed his hand, palm out, three times. Fifteen minutes to go before the arrival of our bus and the trip back to Haphouse.

My spirits lifted when I noticed, threading the fringe, a rescuer from the school. The waitress, softened perhaps by Bauer's generous tip and a pledge never to return, had placed a call on our behalf.

Gil LaFleur, our school psychologist, had arrived in his new car. Rounding out the rescue party, a policeman appeared. He made some cursory inquiries, all the while eyeing the oasis of the morning diner. Failing to uncover any evidence of wrong doing the officer leveled us each in turn with a stern gaze, a warning to remember to walk the line. Then he disappeared inside, perhaps for coffee and a Greek omelet.

Collis raged on. He strained to break my hold, tendons in his neck popping with the effort. Finally, after what seemed like hours, our yellow Bluebird arrived. Wrestling Collis onto a bus carrying a dozen other students returning from job training at the super market or a social outing at the bowling alley, was now out of the question. Jimmy, who had lost interest, was judged calm enough to board for the short trip back to school. The crowd melted away, the bus wheeled out of the parking lot and we were left breathing blue diesel smoke.

We stood dithering on Eureka Avenue, Collis alone among us blessed with a clarity born of absolute certainty. Finally, LaFleur slid behind the wheel of his car and Bauer and I folded into the back seat, Collis struggling between us, a sad sandwich of chagrin.

Once in the car, anticipating a return to school, Collis began to calm down. LaFleur eased us into traffic, Gallic nose and rueful eyes framed in the lozenge of the rearview mirror. In the moments before our clown car maneuver-in-reverse back at Six Stars, we had quietly agreed that Collis should be taken home. In his agitated state, a return to school could guarantee an afternoon of wooly mayhem. We ought to have known better and in fact we did. Collis's love for school was matched only by his hatred for the Ragland Regional Center.

Like all Haphouse students, Collis knew his bus route by heart. Veering right on red, accelerating out of the turn, LaFleur steered us away from Haphouse and toward Ragland. All hell broke loose.

It's funny, the questions that go through your head when someone's trying mightily to bite off your ear. Reattachment. Is it a realistic option? What's the latest scuttlebutt on transplant research? Do they maintain a donor database?

Collis had been tipped murderous by our shameful betrayal. With the windows up the fuggy air grew dense, sour perspiration fogging the glass as we sped out Pennsylvania Road. Collis had managed to scoot down low in the seat onto his head and shoulders, exposing us to a thresher of churning legs, determined to drive a foot through the roof. LeFleur turned and said "Guys, watch my moon roof!"

The lunar reference only heightened the absurdity of our predicament. I began laughing hysterically, the chorus of an old song running through my head. *Buffalo gals, won't you come out tonight? Come out tonight, come out tonight? Buffalo gals, won't you come out tonight, and dance by the light of the moon.*

Alerted by a call from Haphouse, four burley men emerged from cottage number 6 as the car lurched to a stop. Disgorged, we tumbled to the pavement like disappointing prizes from an upended box of Cracker Jack. Collis was whisked away as neatly as if he'd been raptured up by Hell's Angels, the only soul saved amongst sinners.

Haldol isn't used much anymore in favor of improved anti-psychotic medications. The drug is well and rapidly absorbed with a high bioavailability when injected intramuscularly. Bauer, LaFleur and I slipped through the door just before it banged shut. All was silent, residents dispersed to mandatory day programs except for the shrieks coming from a cinder block room down the hall.

We found Collis tied to his bed in four-point restraint, a nice round score good enough to snag him a dubious consolation prize. The injection worked quickly. Within minutes his features softened and his ragged breathing eased. I found an empty room at the end of the hall, sat down on the cold tile floor, and took a deep breath. Just like that, I began to sob uncontrollably. Through hot tears, runny nose slicking my upper lip, I noticed a framed photo of the governor, bolted to the wall. He smiled down at me as if to say, chin up pardner. We've all had days like this.

I'll always remember the coat. Those flapping tails of grace. During all the commotion it had gotten tossed into a corner along with his pants and one untied shoe, nothing more than articles of lifeless clothing. But it was an article of faith with him, his coat. Amulets in the pockets, Collis Flowers Sharpied in the collar and the busted zipper, an elevator forever marooned in the basement.

## Lillo Way
### *APRIL FIRST*

my saint's day   this fool
personal patron o' mine
fine follied fool
feckless feathered fool
cuckoo   cuckold   should you

google fool   dear reader
Victorian fool   Shakespearian
fool   you will find my great uncle
there Wikipedia'd   the self-claimed Sir
William F. Wallett of Derbyshire

I've sprung from a motley's prat
little wonder I've tripped over this
spilled there   blabbed that   left
foot prancing in my mouth
and even at this moment

I'm bounding onto a postage stamp stage
tights proscenium-snagged and running
red flannel coxcomb bells
tinkling my hat's end's donkey's ears
to wish you

a hey nonny nonny jolly April foolscap morn

## Todd Mercer
### *RUST BELT ANNIVERSARY*
#### (Kalabama County, Michigan)

In the winter of our discount tent
we were miserably cold, two fools too proud
to find a way back into indoor living.
The circle of radiated warmth off a wood campfire
isn't many feet across. We stared into each other
over those flames, at times
not speaking, at times speaking
far too much. The forest provided
fuel enough to melt ice, but insufficient
protection for digits subtracted by frostbite.
The ground called me down. It had me burrow deep
under the skin of surplus canvas.
In the winter when we punted, when
we had enough toes to punt, when we fenced
the property but didn't build a home.

## Karen Anderson
### *BLESSINGS*

If you come up short on blessings
consider wealth your spendthrift
grandfather could not plunder. Consider
plunder. Plunge and thunder exactly
matched. Spendthrift exactly else.

We are beholden, I tell you, for a word
like beholden. Heft and vintage.
Riches we did not earn cannot exhaust
fraught with inklings. No way
to put on the kibosh, origin unknown.

If you think this far-fetched think
of far-fetched. Charm and chime enough
to sabotage the taciturn send them
skylarking. Downloads notwithstanding
technology hasn't the wherewithal.

Plethora of blessings. Whatnots
whose whereabouts never forsake.
Your sake mine. Ardent emanations
for the taking tasting toasting.
Giving thanks for the whole shebang.

## Diane Henningfeld
### *WISCONSIN TRIOLET: MY FUTURE MOTHER-IN-LAW TEACHES ME TO PLAY SHEEPSHEAD*

> *At a table of skilled [Sheepshead] players, each card played is both a tactic and a statement. Sometimes the information carried by a card is more important than what the card actually achieves, and sometimes what the card achieves has little to do with the points it takes or gives. It is a game in which there is almost always a right play and a wrong play; few choices are indifferent.*
> —Control Group, Kuro5hin.org

In Sheepshead, you never know your partner
until the cards are played. See a Jack,
that's the partner. Lead trump if you're the partner,
fail if you're not. You never know the partner
until the cards are played. Sometimes it's smarter
to pick the cards. Sometimes you pass. Fact:
in Sheepshead, you never know your partner
until the cards are played. See the Jack?

In the blind? In your hand? Never tell.
Queens, Jacks, diamonds, carry weight, all are trump.
You'll never know your partner very well.
You picked the Jack in the blind? Don't tell.
Listen, girl: playing cards is how we tell
if you belong. Aces, kings, and tens bump
up your points. Feeling blind? Never tell.
In Sheepshead, you'll need diamonds, you'll need trump.

## Greg Jensen
### *SKIN*

I count on it
to take me in
the envelope of space
with a feather in my vest
to remind me flying
is relative.

All secrets are thinly veiled
but once they are punctured
there is no way to put
their logic back inside.
I dreamed a nail
was in my foot.
When I pulled it out
the pain was worse.

I want to touch
something hidden in skin.
I want to separate
and hold on with determined muscles.

A sharp blade finds it
easy to peel away
a layer.

# Kelley Jean White
## *SICK LITTLE PEACH GIRL*

Today. This morning. And she's Autumn's child. First thing and in the morning. Not clear how much her mother is thinking. But it's classic. Nine pound weight loss over a month but really over a week in a seven year old. I can't smell ketones. I just not have that portion of the sense of smell. But others can. She's pale. Pasty. I want to say anything but what I have to say. Well. I'll say what's to say well. It's treatable. She'll feel better with treatment. It's better than some other things it might have been. Really. Some reassurance. And then oh but Christmas was good. And she went to school yesterday. But didn't stay. How cold she was. There's no smile on this child except when she mentions breakfast. Peaches and no syrup in them. They are in water. Why did I even ask that? Yes. Just a smile with peaches. Her mother doesn't seem that worried. She's even dressed for work. Am I having trouble hearing? Well here I am and my children are healthy and I think safe. But I take turns worried about them. And no grandchildren. There are addictions. And no work for a year. And then another one in love. In love with peaches. Peace. And my grotesqueness. And this child has to go. To the Emergency Room. And its pitiful. Face facts. Can't call the diagnosis back. It's pitiful face and pitiful and what is to be my answer.

## Ed Coletti
### *MARIONETTE*

When told that you feel
manipulated by me, I sense
myself your puppeteer, you
my little wooden-headed

marionette moving jerkily
beneath my hand hovering.
How could you, so assertive,
declare yourself lifelessly

available to be so moved?
But once again, I take up
the imputed other role
than whoever I am today,

shrinking a bit more each time
I accept this part for myself
who only wants to make it all
right, once, always, and for all.

## Ed Coletti
### *HYPATIA OF ALEXANDRIA*

She is only a woman.
She is taken with a mere idea.
She contains and delivers it.

Holy men cannot fathom this.
Holy men abort this basal conception.
Holy men shun the texture of selfhood. —

Imagine yourself a 5th century Alexandrian man —

Hypatia blaspheming about harmony,
Hypatia pretender to ownership,
Hypatia speaking of rights

Heresy enrages 5th century holy men
like yourself; so what do you do?
Brand her a pagan to flay and to burn.

She who claimed ownership.
She who described oneness,
She who died complete.

## Elaine McIntosh
### *THE GREEN DRESS*

hidden in shadow
buried in my closet.
soft long sleeved velvet,
draped at my shoulder
swaying skirt to the floor
clinging gently to a body
which outgrew its silhouette
more than twenty years ago.
It is the only dress I ever bought
just because I loved it;
elegant,
simple--
two years after
my husband died
when I could not
remember
soft
or simple
or being wrapped
in anything.

## Ellen Stone
### *MILK PITCHER*

Granny's milk pitcher, squat jug,
songbird blue, simple as a patch
of sky through trees leafed out
in spring. Into the curved lip,
she poured enough milk for supper
from the tin pail in the Frigidaire.
Grandpa never said thank you,
but he praised God in tones solemn
as bullfrogs' songs from the swamp.
Her pitcher sat in the china closet
resting on doilies draped triangular,
sharp as crystal edges. When she
opened the glass doors to show us,
Granny held the pitcher with awe.
As if she were blessed to own
anything. As if sky had come
to dwell in her house for the day.

## Stefen Holtrey
### *TO JOHN KEATS*

We had a tool shed
down by the water and
one day it washed away.
One of those big summer storms.

The ocean took the pieces
but where the shed had been,
a man remained.
He seemed fine, well-dressed if a bit old fashioned
but he just sat there
on the exposed concrete,
looking out at the water.
I never asked why he was there,
and he never spoke a word to me.

One evening, couple months later, I went down
and built another shed over him. Winter was coming in,
and the spray from the waves must have been freezing.

## Ellen Stone
### *DRIVING TO GALESBURG*

Mother says okay, okay
all across the prairie
steadying herself,
her brain wrapping
around white barns, silos,
distance like black locust
fence posts or this barbed
wire gathering in the sheep.

These barns look new
she says, & I say, no.
No, they have always
been here thinking
of her sliding
across years, slipping
by. These numbered
markers tracking us.

It's so huge, she gasps.
Of the sea of corn.
Of the sky's tumult.
Of the grassy, plumey
world, waving & wind-
whipped, a wild mare.
Frayed mane, tail glowing
behind her like a flag,
or some kind of signal.

## Diane Henningfeld
*TURNING*

In March, we drag the stoneboat
through the fields and gather rocks
turned up by frost. Dad's gone.
Rabecki rents the eighty acres

for his oats and beans.
Mother lives alone. She says
she'll never leave the farm.
We turn our eyes away, and keep

the farmyard neat: no broken
plows, or rusty cars, or tools.
The stones we pile behind
the shed, like promises to Dad

we meant to keep. Now,
there's nothing we can keep for long,
not barn, not house, not stones.
We gather at the farm in late

November, raking leaves
wept down by aching oaks. Our bundled
kids run wild across
the lawn and burrow in the leaves

like woodchucks seeking shelter
for their winter sleep. At dusk
we light the bonfire, warm
our hands, talk about the price

of wheat, and drink our bitter
German beer. The sparks fly upward.
High above, migrant
geese form cryptic hieroglyphs.

Mother says she talks to ghosts.
The stones are silent, still.

## Kathleen Diane Nolan
### *BRASS*

It took days to empty
the closets in my mother's house
before she moved
to her new condominium,
beige and uncomplicated.
We filled Hefty bags
with her halter tops and palazzo pants,
with sweater sets and pencil skirts
and high heels. We dragged the bags
to the pile in the garage,
stacked paperbacks
and record albums for Goodwill,
even Herb Alpert and the Tijuana Brass
had to go. That record was always spinning
on the turntable in the den,
my bottle-blonde mother
moving from room to room, her hands
erasing traces of grime
from baseboards and walls,
her hands in soapy water washing glasses
and plates, her wedding ring resting
on the windowsill.
She always saved the ironing
for late afternoon,
poured a glass of Chardonnay
and turned the volume up.
Wrinkles pressed
out of sleeves and collars
with hot steam, starched shirt
after starched shirt
hung over the doorknob,
sips of wine, the sway of her hips,
trumpet notes rising, rising.

# Robert Earle
## *NO REGRETS?*

Eve asked Charles to go get the special cupcakes in Georgetown for dessert Saturday evening. He saw a line in front of the shop and up the hill and called home. Were they were worth the trouble? Eve said yes, they were the best cupcakes in D.C. "Everyone knows that."

Charles looked at everyone who knew what he didn't know. Most of them didn't look like him. Students and regressing young professionals, hats on backward, smart phones to their ears, maybe straight, maybe gay, international, metro, millennial, whatever came next.

On reaching the shop's front corner, he noticed a vacant building down M Street with a For Lease sign. The sight startled him; it wasn't a building that should be empty or dressed-up for luring a franchise; its bricks should be time-blackened and loose, not freshly pointed and painted yellow. Two mid-twenties girls had been shuffling behind him for the last fifteen minutes. He asked if they knew that building had been a music dive from the 60s into the 80s.

"No, I'm from Montreal, here doing research," the brunette said.

The honey blonde said, "I'm her cousin, visiting from Vermont."

A heavy fellow in a George Washington University sweatshirt two spots ahead said, "I heard Taj Mahal there. Like like sitting in his lap."

The girls didn't know about Taj Mahal.

Charles said, "Had about thirty tables, tiny stage, Eric Anderson, John Hammond, probably a lot of people you don't know. Tom Rush? 'No Regrets'?"

"Sing it," the Vermonter said.

Charles wouldn't dare. The heavy guy took the cue. Wasn't bad.

The brunette from Montreal asked who didn't have regrets?

The Vermonter said, "Like, too many to count."

The Montrealer said, "There wouldn't be a word for it otherwise, would there?"

The singer drifted back to join them. He had silver hair and a ponytail and introduced himself: "Paunchy Pancho, or just Paunchy works. I'd have to move from the neighborhood to stop buying these cupcakes."

"One won't hurt," the Montrealer said. Her name was Jessica. Linda, the honey blonde, was her cousin.

"I'm not planning on eating just one. Scarf down a dozen by tomorrow morning. Two before I'm home."

Charles said, "If I came home with one fewer than a dozen for dinner, my wife would kill me. Six people, two for each." He pictured them and their friends, loaded on wine, gray-haired and puffy, telling stories about when they met, what they didn't know then, what they shouldn't have done. It made him sad, the default feeling when he had feelings at all. Eve's dinner parties depressed him, why he drank so much and then would bleed the alcohol out of him in the gym.

Jessica said, "But you've got to have one immediately. The icing! We'll buy one for you."

"How about me?" Paunchy asked.

"You, too," Jessica said.

"For singing," Linda said. "What else do you know?"

Paunchy made the girls laugh with, "Going to move to the country, paint my mailbox blue" and "Daddy's on the rooftop, won't come down."

Charles remembered cramming into The Cellar Door decades ago. Eve in law school, him chumping around D.C. TV stations doing sound.

"More," Linda urged Paunchy.

Paunchy gave her John Prine's "Angel from Montgomery," lamenting nothing to hold onto . . . such a hard way to go.

Jessica said, "I'm researching intergenerational miscommunication--mainly political issues and rhetoric. S'why I find this so interesting, the cultural dimension ten blocks from The White House? Did political people get this?"

"You must be kidding."

"Look, I come three generations later from Canada," Jessica said.

"Joni Mitchell and Neil Young were Canadian, too."

Paunchy sang riffs from "A Case of You" and "Heart of Gold" in a weirdly effective falsetto. He said this music and cupcakes were his life. What if he shared his cupcakes with them in his place up the street and played them some vinyls? The girls looked at one another. It was funny. An old guy's shameless pick-up.

"Okay," Linda said.

"You, too," Paunchy said to Charles. "Share the wealth."

They bought Paunchy's dozen and Charles's dozen and followed Paunchy to his house up 33rd Street. He was a tax attorney, divorced yet still wealthy. The whole place, four stories, was his. He started spinning disks. Jessica got out her notepad and asked what each song meant to Charles and Paunchy, who were fifty-nine and sixty-three respectively. They recalled where they'd first heard it, who they were with, what was going on in the world, who was president. Did the songs make them feel free? she asked. No, not free, escaped, Paunchy said. But soon to be caught, Charles said.

"Now sing us some Stan Rogers," Paunchy said.

"I don't know him," Jessica said.

"How about Leonard Cohen?"

Jessica began singing "Suzanne" in a pretty soprano voice. She caught the sadness of the half crazy woman by the river.

Paunchy mixed up a pitcher of brandy, champagne and bitters he said would complement the remaining cupcakes perfectly. Linda said the cupcakes with their thick frosting already were perfect, but he was right. Likewise he was right when the cupcakes were gone and it was just the cocktails and his strong little Schimmelpenninck cigars, which Charles hadn't smoked since those days in the Door, that's what they called it, the Door. You didn't have to knock, no reservations, just let yourself in. He started telling the girls about listening to the music Paunchy was playing while stoned. That, in itself, was like an escape hatch for his entire generation.

"Getting stoned really mattered?" Jessica asked. "Because it was new or because everything was happening at once?"

Charles said culture and politics swamped one another when you were stoned, you couldn't tell one from the other, white from black, sex from war, night from day. Linda said her parents said that.

Jessica laughed. "Meanwhile Canadians were watching you in horror. Americans screaming at each other, and then... this is my next project, Quebec begins screaming: Let us go! Separatism! Sovereignty! We want out! What did all this tearing everything apart mean?"

Paunchy said, "It meant we found out how much we hated our parents and vice-versa. My father didn't want me in the house. Ten years I wasn't."

Everyone began finishing one another's sentences about hate, taboos, and what difference did it make, speaking in English or speaking in French? They grew tipsy. Paunchy kept the music going, Charles said he never got out of the techie rut, never became his own boss, spent half his life unemployed living off his lawyer wife.

Jessica put her notebook down and touched his face. She was crying on his behalf. "No, no," she said. "I was wrong. I do know that song about regrets, but in French, Edith Piaf sang it, 'Non, je ne regrette rien.'"

"Rush ripped it off?" Charles asked.

"Maybe he just covered it," Paunchy said. "He came from New Hampshire," he told Linda, "not far from you."

Jessica was singing slowly, beautifully capturing Piaf's commitment to regretting nothing. "'Not the good things that have been done to me,'" she translated, "'or the bad things, they're all the same to me.'" Then she asked if Paunchy had any Edith Piaf. Of course. Soundtrack music from *Saving Private Ryan*:

> *Nous nous aimions bien tendrement,*
> *Comme s'aiment tous les amants*

"What's it mean?" Linda asked Jessica.

"'We loved each other tenderly...like we loved all lovers...'"

Linda asked the men, "In your experience, do all lovers love one another tenderly?"

Charles and Paunchy looked at one another. Should they lie and say they always loved tenderly or tell the truth and risk the moment?

Finally Paunchy said, "Not tenderly enough. How about you two?"

The cousins, in their mid-twenties, hesitated, knowing they were on the edge of having loved so many times so foolishly that they'd never love like that again.

"It would be a stretch to say that," Jessica said. She was stocky, busty, and strong-browed. Her turtleneck was tight. Her brown hair gleamed. When she spoke French, or sang it, she was elegant and soulful. In English, she was firm, a realist. "You sing because not everything goes tenderly."

"What does tenderly mean to you?" Charles asked her.

"It's cherishing the fact that you'll never have enough time for each other," Jessica said. "Eternity wouldn't be enough time."

"I don't know women like this," Charles said.

"But you know men like this," Linda said.

"Who?"

"You."

"Me?"

Had she been looking at Charles in a way no one noticed? Was he now looking at her in the same way?

"Look, I'm an insurance adjustor in Vermont, and I never have conversations like this," she said. "Then I come to D.C. to visit Jessica and within twenty-four hours I hear and think about more interesting things than I have in years. What, you're thirteen, fourteen, when you first ask what is tender, what is love? Yet you still do."

"Still," Charles said, mocking himself.

They were rattled, all of them. Too much brandy, too much smoke, the afternoon light dying so that it was getting hard to see one another, releasing the honesty of strangers who could afford to tell the truth because they'd never be together again.

"What about dinner? Let's go out," Paunchy said.

Jessica said, "I want Afghan. How about everyone else?"

"There's an Afghan place I know. Ten minutes we're there," Paunchy said.

Charles almost agreed. Then he remembered the cupcakes, Eve cooking, the dinner. He said he couldn't do it. Paunchy said to call Eve and have her bring everyone along. Charles thought about the days when he would have tried this, not succeeded, but tried. Now he didn't. He bade them goodnight. All three hugged him. Jessica, not Linda, was the one who kissed him on the cheek. Paunchy was on the phone recruiting another guy even before Charles got out the door. He seemed to be having success.

"Yeah, the Khyber Pass in a half-hour. No, don't dress up, casual." Charles heard no more as he stepped down onto the brick sidewalk beside a gas lamp and stopped a moment, trying to remember where he'd parked the car. P and 34th. He walked over there and carefully placed the box in the passenger footwell so that the cupcakes wouldn't slide into one another and spoil their thick crowns of icing as he crossed the Key Bridge. Eve would notice immediately he'd been drinking and smoking and ask how that could happen getting cupcakes. But if he explained, if he told everyone at dinner, no one would like hearing how much it filled him with regret he'd come home.

# ACKNOWLEDGEMENTS

"Bullets Pass Through" by Dave Hardin references lyrics from "Buffalo Gals," a song written and published in 1884 as "Lubly Fan," by minstrel John Hodges, who performed under the name "Cool White."

"No Regrets" by Robert Earle references lyrics from "Non, je ne regrette rien," a French song composed by Charles Dumont in 1956 and recorded by Edith Piaf in 1960.

# CONTRIBUTOR NOTES

*JEFFREY ALFIER is winner of the 2014 Kithara Book Prize for his poetry collection, *Idyll for a Vanishing River* (Glass Lyre Press, 2013). His latest work is *The Color of Forgiveness*, a poetry collaboration with Tobi Alfier (Mojave River Review Press). He is also author of *The Storm Petrel – Poems of Ireland* (Grayson Books) and *The Wolf Yearling* (Silver Birch Press). He is the founder and co-editor of *San Pedro River Review*.

KAREN ANDERSON earned her MA in English Literature from the University of Michigan. For 30 years she wrote a weekly column for the *Traverse City Record-Eagle* and published two books of her work. She now contributes weekly commentaries to Interlochen Public Radio.

ROBB ASTOR grew up on the shores of Lake Michigan in the small village of Pentwater. His childhood was full of forests, fields, dunes, and summers at his grandmother's farm. He served as a Peace Corps Volunteer in the United Republic of Tanzania. Robb currently lives in Traverse City, Michigan, with his wife and two children. Writing has been a daily habit of Robb's for nearly thirty years. His collection of poetry, *Bitter Dagaa*, was selected for publication by Michigan Writers Cooperative Press in 2014. He is the host of Open Read, a monthly open mic event for poets in the Grand Traverse area.

*ED COLETTI is a poet, painter, fiction writer, and chess player who studied under Robert Creeley in San Francisco (1970-71). Ed recently has had work in *The Brooklyn Rail, North American Review, Hawai'i Pacific Review, Spillway, Ambush Review* and *So It Goes – The Literary Journal of the Kurt Vonnegut Memorial Library*. Recent fiction publications include the *Crucible* Fiction Prize (2nd place), *Noir Nation* and *Romance Magazine*. Internet presence includes "Ed Coletti's P3" and also "No Money In Poetry." His book, *When Hearts Outlive Minds*, was released in June 2011. *Germs, Viruses, and Catechisms* was published by Civil Defense Publications (San Francisco) during Winter 2013. Ed refers to those poems as "historicowarpoligious." He now is working on *Apollo Blue's Harp*, a poetic-history of music.

*ANDREW COLLARD lives in Madison Heights, MI, and attends Oakland University. His poems can be found in *Juked*, *A Minor* and *One Throne*, among others.

With more than seventy stories in print and online literary journals, *ROBERT EARLE is one of the more widely published contemporary writers of short fiction. He also has published two novels (*The Way Home* and *The Man Clothed in Linen*) and two books of nonfiction (*Nights in the Pink Motel: An American Strategist's Pursuit of Peace in Iraq* and *North American Identities: Search for Community*). He lives in Chapel Hill, North Carolina.

DAVE HARDIN is a Michigan poet, fiction writer and artist. His poems have appeared in *3 Quarks Daily*, *The Prague Review*, *Drunken Boat*, *Hermes Poetry Journal*, *Dunes Review*, *Epigraph Magazine*, *Loose Change*, *ARDOR*, *Carolina Quarterly*, *The Madison Review*, the upcoming 2014 *Bear River Review* and others.

*DIANE HENNINGFELD is originally from Ohio, but has lived in Adrian, Michigan for over forty years. She holds a Ph.D. from Michigan State in English. Prior to her retirement in 2012, she taught at Adrian College as a professor of literature and writing, as well as working as a freelance writer and reviewer. Her poems often feature the Great Lakes states, and have appeared in *Storm Cellar*, *The Michigan Writer* and *Penwood Review*.

When *STEFEN HOLTREY isn't making coffee, reading, or writing, he's probably doing handstands. He grew up in Interlochen, Michigan, went to school in a few different places, and he looks forward to what may or may not happen next.

*GREG JENSEN'S poems have appeared in *december*, *Fugue*, *Bodega*, and *Crab Creek Review*. In addition to being a poet, he is a dad, husband, avid bicyclist, and yoga enthusiast who works for a non-profit serving homeless adults on Seattle's original Skid Row. He is currently enrolled in the MFA in Creative Writing program at Pacific University.

*ZILKA JOSEPH was nominated twice for a Pushcart and is a Hopwood award winner. Her work has appeared in *Kenyon Review Online, Quiddity, Review Americana, Gatronomica* and *Cutthroat. Lands I Live In* and *What Dread*, her two chapbooks, were nominated for a PEN America and a Pushcart prize respectively. She is a writing coach and editor, and teaches creative writing in Ann Arbor and in the Metro Detroit area. www.zilkajoseph.com

*Cover artist SKYE LIVINGSTON is an interdisciplinary artist working with textiles, paper, and organic materials. She completed her BFA in 2012 at the Kansas City Art Institute and has received several awards for her work, including an ArtsKC Inspiration Grant in support of her first solo exhibition in 2013. She has exhibited in group shows nationwide and completed several

solo and two-person shows in Kansas City. At the moment she is nomadic, maintaining her studio practice at artist residencies across the country, including the ISLAND Hill House Artist Residency in East Jordan, Michigan.

ELAINE MCINTOSH is a retired nurse-practitioner who relishes the time in the beautiful woods where she lives to be able to write poems stored in her head for many years. Other poems have been published in *Image: The Journal of Nursing Scholarship* and *Huron Review*.

TODD MERCER's digital chapbook, *Life-wish Maintenance* (2015) appeared at Right Hand Pointing. He won the first Woodstock Writers Festival's Flash Fiction contest. His chapbook, *Box of Echoes*, won the Michigan Writers Cooperative Press contest. Mercer's poetry and fiction appear in journals such as *Apocrypha & Abstractions, Blue Collar Review, The Camel Saloon, Camroc Press Review, Cheap Pop, Dunes Review, East Coast Literary Review, Eunoia Review, Gravel, Kentucky Review, Kudzu, The Lake, The Legendary, Lost Coast Review, Main Street Rag Anthologies, Midwestern Gothic, RiverLit, Spartan* and *theNewer York*.

*KATHLEEN DIANE NOLAN is a recent graduate of the MFA in Writing program at Pacific University. Her work has appeared in *Rattle* and she was a semi-finalist for the 2013 Rattle Poetry Prize. She lives in New York City.

*NICCO PANDOLFI lives, works, and writes in Traverse City, Michigan.

*CONSTANCE REINHARD worked as a corporate attorney in Cleveland and Chicago before retiring early to pursue the vocation of writing. She fell in love with northern Michigan as a child, and moved there with her husband after retirement. They spend winters in central Ohio near family. She has studied poetry with Teresa Scollon and fiction with John Pahl. This is her first published poetry.

*SUZANNE ROSENTHAL SHUMWAY was born in Brooklyn, New York, but grew up in Texas. She has a Ph.D. in Victorian literature from The University of Texas at Austin. She writes essays, historical fiction, and literary criticism.

ELLEN STONE teaches at Community High School in Ann Arbor, Michigan. Her chapbook, *The Solid Living World*, was published by Michigan Writers Cooperative Press in 2013. Ellen's poems have appeared recently in *Dunes Review, Melancholy Hyperbole*, and in the anthology, *Uncommon Core*, published by Red Beard Press.

*JULIE STOTZ-GHOSH's work has appeared in various journals and anthologies, including *Quarter After Eight, Poetry Midwest*, and *Sudden Stories: A Mammoth Book of Miniscule Fiction*. She teaches writing and literature at Kalamazoo Valley Community College.

*BRENDAN STRAUBEL earned undergraduate and graduate degrees in English from the University of Missouri-Columbia. He has had poems, fiction and nonfiction published in a variety of local, regional and state publications; however, "Waxwing" is his first submission to any publication in over a decade. He has lived in Benzie County for 16 years and works as RN in the Emergency Department at West Shore Medical Center in Manistee, Michigan.

*LILLO WAY's poems have appeared (or are forthcoming) in *Poet Lore, the Madison Review, the Sow's Ear Poetry Review, Poetry East, Common Ground Review, Tampa Review, Third Wednesday, Yemassee, Freshwater, Quiddity, Santa Fe Literary Review, WomenArts Quarterly, Marathon Literary Review* and *SLAB*, among others. Five of her poems have been anthologized in the "Good Works" series of FutureCycle Press. She has received grants from the NEA, NY State Council on the Arts and the Geraldine R. Dodge Foundation for her choreographic work involving poetry.

Originally from Holland, Michigan, KIRK WESTPHAL is an environmental consultant in Boston. He works around the world on long-range water supply plans. By night, he writes poetry and memoirs. He is a 2012 winner of the Plein Air Poetry Contest in Massachusetts, and his poems have appeared in *Dunes Review, The Road Not Taken, Albatross, National Public Radio*, and the chapbook *Lines in the Landscape*. He is also the author of a nonfiction book entitled *No Ordinary Game: Miraculous Moments in Backyards and Sandlots*, scheduled for publication in June 2015.

*KELLEY WHITE is now a pediatrician in rural New Hampshire after working at a inner-city community health center in Philadelphia for nearly 30 years. She was the recipient of a Pennsylvania Council on the Arts Grant in 2008 just before returning to her home village in the North. Her most recent book is *Two Birds in Flame*, poems related to the Shaker Community in Canterbury, New Hampshire, published by Beech River Books.

*JANICE ZERFAS received her MA and Ph.D in Creative Writing from Western Michigan University and has worked with William Olsen and Nancy Eimers. Her work has been published in some small press magazines such as *Indiana Review, The MacGuffin, Many Mountains Moving, Crazy Horse*, and *The Bear River Review*. She has also participated at the Bear River Writers' Workshop, where she had the pleasure of working with Thomas Lynch. She also once won poetry praise from Gerald Stern.

*denotes first appearance in *Dunes Review*

## Call for Patrons

*Dunes Review* is a not-for-profit endeavor to promote creative work within the Northern Michigan writing community and beyond.

The cost of publication can be underwritten in part by individual contributions. Please support the publication of the Summer/Fall 2015 issue with a donation of $25.

Send your check payable
to Michigan Writers to:

Michigan Writers
P.O. Box 2355
Traverse City, MI 49685

Thank you in advance for your support!

# DUNES REVIEW SUBMISSION GUIDELINES

To help us retain the strong regional identity of our journal, individuals with current Michigan Writers memberships ($40 annually, which includes a two-issue subscription) may submit work at no cost. However, we welcome submissions from anyone, anywhere. If you are not a current member of Michigan Writers, please use the General Submitter category on our Submittable page ($5). Or, join or renew your MW membership. Learn more about MW and the benefits of membership at michwriters.org/join.

All submissions received during the reading periods will be read. The response time will vary according to the number of submissions. We make every effort to respond to all submissions within four months of receipt. If you have submitted work via dunesreview.submittable.com and have not received a response within four months, please contact us by email at dunesreview@michwriters.org. Our next reading period runs from April 15-July 15, 2015.

All submissions must be submitted via dunesreview.submittable.com. We do not accept submissions via email or regular mail. You will need to have a submittable.com account to send work, even if you have previously submitted to *Dunes Review* using other methods. Creating an account is free, and you can easily keep track of your submissions from within your account.

Please submit no more than one submission in a given genre while a decision from us is outstanding; multiple submissions sent in the same genre will be unread. Simultaneous submissions (the same pieces sent to multiple journals) are permitted. Please withdraw your work from Submittable immediately or contact us via email if the work has been accepted elsewhere.

**We consider:**

- short fiction & essays (up to 3000 words)
- poetry (3-5 poems; please format & submit as a single .doc, .docx, or .pdf document, one poem per page)

**We do not accept:**

- unsolicited reviews
- unsolicited interviews
- snail mail or email submissions (please use dunesreview.submittable.com)
- previously published material

**The Fine Print**

When submitting poetry, please group 3-5 poems in a single document and then upload your submission. Do not submit your poems individually; doing so will make your poems appear as multiple poetry submissions, which will not be considered. If you are interested in submitting translations of literary work, please query the editor (dunesreview@michwriters.org) before submitting. The translator is responsible for all author and publisher permissions regarding the source work.

You agree to be added to *Dunes Review* and Michigan Writers email lists when you submit. You may unsubscribe from these lists at any time.

Payment for accepted work comes in the form of two copies of the printed journal.

Publication rights notice: Work published in *Dunes Review* may be reprinted on our website's Archives page. Otherwise, all rights revert to author upon publication.

The regular submission deadline for our next issue (19.2, Summer/Fall 2015) is July 15, 2015. Please "Like" us on Facebook and receive notices for upcoming events and public readings.

## SUBSCRIPTIONS

We encourage you to become a subscriber. To receive two (2) issues, or to give a gift subscription, please send your name, address and a check for $20 to: Dunes Review, P.O. Box 2355, Traverse City, MI 49685. Alternatively, become a member of Michigan Writers ($40 annually) and gain access to other benefits as well as a subscription. Students may become members at the reduced rate of $25/year.

For more information about Michigan Writers membership, activities and events, please visit www.michwriters.org.

**MichiganWriters**

Made in the USA
Charleston, SC
31 March 2015